JESUS MAKES ME NEW

Kids + Family Devotional

THE DAILY GRACE CO.®

When we trust in Jesus
to be our Savior,
God forgives our sins.

WHAT'S INSIDE

Part 6

Part 7

Appendix

When we trust in Jesus
to be our Savior,
God forgives our sins.

HOW TO USE THIS DEVOTIONAL

Hey, grown-ups!

We are so excited that you picked up *Jesus Makes Me New*. This devotional is all about how Jesus forgives our sin and helps us live in ways that please God. Sin can be a tricky subject to talk about with kids. Sometimes, we can be too heavy-handed when we discuss sin with kids and end up making them feel scared or overwhelmed. But we can also treat sin too lightly and water down its seriousness. This devotional is designed to not fall into either one of those traps. Instead, this devotional is meant to help kids understand the reality of their sin but also the reality of our amazing Savior. Our hope is that this devotional will challenge kids in just the right ways while also encouraging them with the good news of the gospel.

This devotional has been designed with the season of Lent in mind, but you don't have to wait until Lent to use it! This is because it has also been designed with flexibility in mind, so you can use it with your kids at any point during the year.

No matter when you decide to begin this resource, let's take a look at what your family can expect to find within its pages.

WHAT TO EXPECT

This devotional is divided into seven sections (titled Parts 1–7) — each to be used during one week of Lent (or whenever else you decide to go through it!). In each section, you will find a memory verse and a few daily devotions, along with a "Gospel Talk" prompt at the end of each section. This is how each of these resources can practically be used:

- Each section begins with a **memory verse** that relates to the content in that section. Practice that memory verse before you begin each daily devotion to help your kids hide God's Word in their hearts (Psalm 119:11) as you work through this devotional.

- You will then come to that section's **daily devotions**. Each daily devotion should take between ten to fifteen minutes to complete. It will include a Scripture reading, a short reflection, two questions to discuss, and two prayer prompts for your family to pray through together.

- Finally, each section ends with a **Gospel Talk**. Each Gospel Talk prompt will provide your family the opportunity to talk through the gospel together in a call-and-response format. Children learn through repetition, and there's no more important truth to repeat to them than the gospel!

Bonus: As a bonus, you can download **a coloring sheet** by scanning the QR code below. This coloring sheet is designed for children to fill in as your family walks through the daily devotions. Each daily devotion will tell you exactly what to color on the coloring page so that by the end of this 40-day resource, you will have a completely colored picture!

COLORING PAGE
QR CODE

Many families will find it beneficial to go through the daily devotions on weekdays and save the Gospel Talks for weekends — but you can feel the freedom to use this resource however works best for your family's unique rhythms!

IF YOU DECIDE TO USE THIS RESOURCE DURING LENT . . .

We encourage you to use the content on pages 12–14 to help your kids understand the purpose of Lent and why you are doing this devotional with them during this unique time in the church calendar. In addition, you will find a Lent schedule on page 15 that will show you how to fit this devotional perfectly into the Lenten season.

IF YOU ARE NOT USING THE DEVOTIONAL DURING LENT . . .

Then simply work through it at a pace that works for you and your family!

We hope that *Jesus Makes Me New* will be a helpful discipleship tool for your family. And we pray that this devotional will stir your family's affection for Jesus and open hearts to receive the good news of the gospel!

New to family discipleship? Find some tried-and-true tips for making the most of your family's devotional time on pages 112–119.

WHAT IS LENT?

The season of Lent can be a wonderful time to introduce your children to the truths of the gospel and help them see their need for a Savior. In fact, that's why we designed this family devotional! Though it can be used any time of the year, it makes the perfect Lenten companion for your family.

If you choose to use this resource during Lent, it can be helpful to start by taking a few moments to better understand this unique season in the church calendar. So, let's take a quick look at Lent: its history, how it is commonly observed today, and how this specific devotional can fit into your family's Lenten practice.

THE HISTORY OF LENT

The Church began observing the season of Lent as a way to help Christians intentionally prepare their hearts for the celebration of Easter. Lent is forty days long (excluding Sundays), and it begins on Ash Wednesday and concludes on Holy Saturday. Historically, it has been observed as a time for believers to be devoted to prayer and fasting.

HOW LENT IS OBSERVED TODAY

Interestingly, the structure of Lent has varied through the years. In the past, the forty days of Lent involved prayer and fasting from a particular food. The idea behind this fasting is to reflect Jesus's forty days of fasting in the wilderness before beginning His ministry (Luke 4:1–13).

However, in our current day and age, what people choose to give up during Lent is their own choice: some may give up a type of food, while others may give up a tangible item or a form of technology. Either way, the choice to give something up reflects a believer's desire to make some sort of sacrifice. Like sacrificing food, we give up something that we often rely upon so that we can rely wholeheartedly on the Lord. When we feel pulled toward that thing we have given up, we are reminded to depend on the Lord above all things.

However, we must not see whatever sacrifice we make during Lent as the means to earn God's salvation. Rather, sacrifices during Lent are a response to the salvation we have received through Christ. As we sacrifice, we are reminded of the sacrifice Jesus made for our sake. Even if you do not choose to give something up, Lent is still a special time that points you to Jesus.

The season of Lent can be a wonderful time to introduce your children to the truths of the gospel.

In addition to fasting during Lent, many people take time to reflect on their sins. Often, what someone chooses to give up during Lent is connected to a particular sinful habit they wish to remove or change. And while it is not wrong to reflect on and seek to remove sin during Lent, it is possible to go about Lent with the incorrect posture. For example, some may view Lent as a time to temporarily keep themselves away from something "bad" until they can pick it back up again after Lent. In fact, this is why many people view the holiday Mardi Gras (which takes place the day before Lent begins) as a time to indulge in whatever they can before stopping for the forty days of Lent.

How To Use This Devotional During Lent

This resource provides content for each day of the Lenten season, excluding Sundays. This includes a daily devotion for each of the week-days leading up to Easter, a "Gospel Talk" prompt for each Saturday, and rest days on Sundays. Use the built-in rest days to take a break from the devotional material, practice your memory verse, or catch up on missed devotions.

To learn more about the structure and format of this devotional, turn to page 8.

The calendar on the next page maps out a schedule of content your family can follow each day to complete the study by Easter Sunday.

Lent Schedule

CALENDAR DAY	STUDY DAY	CALENDAR DAY	STUDY DAY
Ash Wednesday	1	Monday	23
Thursday	2	Tuesday	24
Friday	3	Wednesday	25
Saturday	4	Thursday	26
Sunday	R*	Friday	27
Monday	5	Saturday	28
Tuesday	6	Sunday	R
Wednesday	7	Monday	29
Thursday	8	Tuesday	30
Friday	9	Wednesday	31
Saturday	10	Thursday	32
Sunday	R	Friday	33
Monday	11	Saturday	34
Tuesday	12	Sunday	R
Wednesday	13	Monday	35
Thursday	14	Tuesday	36
Friday	15	Wednesday	37
Saturday	16	Thursday	38
Sunday	R	Friday	39
Monday	17	Saturday	40
Tuesday	18	Easter Sunday	41
Wednesday	19		
Thursday	20		
Friday	21		
Saturday	22		
Sunday	R		

*Rest day

PART 1

Memory Verse

For while we were still
helpless, at the right time,
Christ died for the ungodly.

ROMANS 5:6

Our Sin Problem

MEMORY VERSE

For while we were still helpless, at the right
time, Christ died for the ungodly.

Romans 5:6

READ TOGETHER

Romans 3:23–24

Jesus died on the cross for our sin. But what is sin? Sin is when we disobey God. The Bible says that *everybody* — not just some people! — have disobeyed God and deserve to be punished. But this is why God sent Jesus! Jesus is God's Son who came to earth, died on the cross, and rose again. On the cross, Jesus was punished for our sin. And when we trust in Jesus to be our Savior, God forgives our sins.

How amazing is Jesus? Jesus did not have to die for us on the cross. He is the one person who never sinned. But He chose to die for our sin because He loves us so much! Even though our sin is bad, we have a great Savior who takes our sin away.

Even though our sin is bad, we have a great Savior who takes our sin away.

- What is sin?

- Would you want to be punished for what somebody else did wrong? Why do you think Jesus was willing to be punished for your sins?

- **THANK** God for forgiving our sin through Jesus.

- **ASK** for God to help you remember His love and live in obedience to Him.

Optional: Color all the number 1's on the bonus coloring sheet.
Note: The numbers go through 40. There are 6 spots to color for each number.

Where Sin Came From

MEMORY VERSE

For while we were still helpless, at the right
time, Christ died for the ungodly.
Romans 5:6

READ TOGETHER

Genesis 1:31, Genesis 3:15

When God created our world, every part of it was good! There was no sadness, sickness, or death. And He put the first people, Adam and Eve, in a garden full of beautiful trees they could eat food from. There was one tree they couldn't eat from, but other than that, Adam and Eve were told to enjoy God and the world He made.

But instead of listening to God, they listened to the words of Satan. Satan told them they couldn't trust God and that they should eat from the tree they weren't supposed to eat from. Adam and Eve believed Satan's lies and disobeyed God. As a consequence, now the world is full of sadness, sickness, and death.

But God promised to send Someone who would one day take away sin and death: Jesus! Jesus came to earth many years later and died on the cross to save us from our sin. And He promises to one day remove sin forever so that we can live with Him in a world that is perfect!

God promised To send Someone who would one day Take away sin and death. Jesus!

- What lie did Satan tell Adam and Eve about God?

- How has God been good to us as a family?

PRAY TOGETHER

- **THANK** God for being good and creating a beautiful world.

- **ASK** God to help you remember that He always wants what is best for you.

Optional: Color all the number 2's on the bonus coloring sheet.

Note: The numbers go through 40. There are 6 spots to color for each number.

Jesus Makes Us New

MEMORY VERSE

For while we were still helpless, at the right
time, Christ died for the ungodly.
Romans 5:6

READ TOGETHER

Galatians 5:22–23

The Bible gives good news and bad news. The bad news is that everybody sins, and people who sin deserve God's punishment. But the good news is that God saves us from our sin. Out of His great love, God gave us Jesus. Through Jesus, our sins are forgiven, and God gives us eternal life.

But God does not only forgive our sins. He also helps us start living in ways that please Him. We will still struggle with sin. But Jesus makes us new by giving us His Holy Spirit, who helps us love God and obey His commands. Like how trees grow fruit, the Spirit grows "fruit" — or good works — in our lives. He helps us love God more and more and love sin less and less. This means that God doesn't save us because we've obeyed Him; we obey Him because He has saved us!

God doesn't save us because we've obeyed Him; we obey Him because He has saved us!

- What does the Holy Spirit help us do?

- What are some examples of ways that we could love God more than sin?

- **THANK** God for His forgiveness and the gift of the Holy Spirit.

- **ASK** for the Spirit to help you love God more and sin less.

Optional: Color all the number 3's on the bonus coloring sheet.

Note: The numbers go through 40. There are 6 spots to color for each number.

Gospel Talk

MEMORY VERSE

For while we were still helpless, at the right
time, Christ died for the ungodly.
Romans 5:6

Let's practice speaking the gospel to one another. Why? Because the gospel is the best news we could ever hear! And the more we talk about it, the better we will understand just how wonderful it is!

Grown-up: Who sins?
Kids: Everyone sins.

Grown-up: What happens because of our sin?
Kids: We are separated from God forever.

Grown-up: Can we get rid of our sin on our own?
Kids: No!

Grown-up: Who can save us from our sin?
Kids: Jesus!

Grown-up: What should we do to be saved?
Kids: Confess our sin and believe in Jesus as our Savior.

Grown-up: What does it mean to be saved?
Kids: Our sin is forgiven, and we are a part of God's family forever!

PRAY TOGETHER

- **THANK** God that He saves us from our sin.

- **ASK** God to help you understand the good news of the gospel.

Optional: Color all the number 4's on the bonus coloring sheet.
Note: The numbers go through 40. There are 6 spots to color for each number.

PART 2

Memory Verse

He said to him, "Love the Lord your God with all your heart, with all your soul, and with all your mind."

MATTHEW 22:37

Confessing Our Sin

MEMORY VERSE

He said to him, "Love the Lord your God with all your heart, with all your soul, and with all your mind."
Matthew 22:37

READ TOGETHER

1 John 1:9

When we disobey someone, we should tell them we're sorry and ask them to forgive us. We should also tell God we're sorry anytime we sin. We shouldn't hide what we did from God. Instead, we should be honest about what we did wrong. This is called confessing. And this can feel scary! It's never fun to admit to someone that we did something wrong.

But the good news is that God promises to forgive our sins when we confess them to Him! And since God forgives our sins through Jesus, we don't have to be scared of confessing our sins to Him. Sometimes when we sin, we might think that God is angry and doesn't want to talk to us. But that's not true at all. God is loving and forgiving, and He wants us to come to Him. We can be honest with God when we sin and enjoy His forgiveness.

God promises to forgive our sins when we confess them to Him!

- Is it hard for you to admit that you've done something wrong?

- What are ways that we as a family have disobeyed God recently?

- **THANK** God that we can confess our sins to Him, knowing that He accepts us.

- **ASK** that God would help us obey Him and not hide from Him when we sin.

Optional: Color all the number 5's on the bonus coloring sheet.

Note: The numbers go through 40. There are 6 spots to color for each number.

Loving God First

MEMORY VERSE

He said to him, "Love the Lord your God with all your
heart, with all your soul, and with all your mind."
Matthew 22:37

READ TOGETHER
Matthew 22:37–38

God created us to love Him more than anything. But we often love other things more than God. And anything we love more than God is called an idol. In the Old Testament, idols were often statues of fake gods. Lots of people worshiped fake gods, but God told His people to be different and worship only Him, the one true God. Sadly, His people didn't always listen, and they often chose fake gods over the real God.

We also worship idols today, though our idols aren't usually statues of fake gods. Instead, our idols are usually things like our video games or toys — things that give us happiness for a short amount of time. But God gives us happiness that can't be taken away.

When we worship idols, we miss out on the true happiness God gives us. Thankfully, Jesus gives us new hearts that want to worship God! With the help of the Holy Spirit, we can love God more than anything else!

God gives us happiness that can't be taken away.

- What is an idol?

- What are some things that we, as a family, might be tempted to love more than God?

- **THANK** God that we can find true, lasting happiness in Him.

- **ASK** God to help you love Him more than anything else, even things that are good.

Optional: Color all the number 6's on the bonus coloring sheet.

Note: The numbers go through 40. There are 6 spots to color for each number.

Being Holy Like God is Holy

MEMORY VERSE

He said to him, "Love the Lord your God with all your heart, with all your soul, and with all your mind."
Matthew 22:37

READ TOGETHER

1 Peter 1:14–15, 18–19

All of us have people we look up to and admire. And since we admire them, we want to imitate them because we want to be like them! In the same way, God wants us to imitate Him. When we become Christians, we join God's family. God becomes our heavenly Father, and we become His children. And God wants His children to imitate Him in all that we think, say, and do. He tells us to be holy since He is holy.

To be holy means to be set apart and pure. Only God is perfectly holy, but we can imitate God's holiness by obeying Him. We can choose to do what God says to do instead of sinning. The more we obey God, the more we will grow in holiness. And as we grow in holiness, we will look more like our holy God!

The more we obey God, the more we will grow in holiness.

- Who are some people you admire and try to imitate? What do you admire about them?

- What are some ways we can imitate God together as a family?

- **THANK** God for being a God worth imitating!

- **ASK** that God would help us imitate what He is like.

Optional: Color all the number 7's on the bonus coloring sheet.
Note: The numbers go through 40. There are 6 spots to color for each number.

Following Jesus

He said to him, "Love the Lord your God with all your heart, with all your soul, and with all your mind."
Matthew 22:37

Matthew 9:9

Jesus wants us to follow Him. This means that instead of doing what *we* want to do, we do what *He* wants us to do! And how do we know what Jesus wants us to do? We know by reading the Bible.

As Christians, we follow Jesus by obeying Him and acting like Him. But following Jesus isn't always easy. Sometimes it's easier to do what *we* want rather than what *Jesus* wants us to do. But God gives us the Holy Spirit to help us follow Him.

Jesus is the best leader to follow. When we follow Jesus with the Spirit's help, we experience joy, peace, and so much more, even when following Him is hard! We miss out on these gifts when we only do what we want to do. So let's follow Jesus and experience the life that He gives us!

When we follow Jesus with the Spirit's help, we experience joy, peace, and so much more.

- Why is it important to follow Jesus?

- When can it be hard to obey Jesus?

PRAY TOGETHER

- THANK God for the joy and peace that Jesus brings to us.

- ASK for God's help to do what Jesus wants us to do instead of what we want to do.

Optional: Color all the number 8's on the bonus coloring sheet.

Note: The numbers go through 40. There are 6 spots to color for each number.

Being a Living Sacrifice

He said to him, "Love the Lord your God with all your heart, with all your soul, and with all your mind."
Matthew 22:37

Romans 12:1

Because God created us and sent Jesus to rescue us from sin, we should worship Him! One way to do this is by singing songs to Him about how great He is. But we can also worship Him by how we live and treat others. When we talk and behave in ways that honor God, the Bible says that we become living sacrifices.

What does it mean to be a living sacrifice? It means that we live in a way that says "thank you" to God for saving us! And Romans 12:1 says we should be living sacrifices because of "the mercies of God." This means that we shouldn't live in ways that honor God just because we *have* to but because we *get* to! The more we are reminded of how much God loves us, the more we will want to please Him with our words, our thoughts, and our behavior.

The more we are reminded of how much God loves us, the more we will want to please Him.

ANSWER TOGETHER

- Why is it important to remember how much God loves us? How can that affect our behavior?

- What are ways we can please God through our actions this week?

PRAY TOGETHER

- **THANK** God for choosing to love us and save us, even though we are sinners.

- **ASK** God to help you to live in ways that please Him.

Optional: Color all the number 9's on the bonus coloring sheet.

Note: The numbers go through 40. There are 6 spots to color for each number.

Gospel Talk

MEMORY VERSE

He said to him, "Love the Lord your God with all your
heart, with all your soul, and with all your mind."
Matthew 22:37

Let's practice speaking the gospel to one another. Why? Because the
gospel is the best news we could ever hear! And the more we talk about
it, the better we will understand just how wonderful it is!

Grown-up: Who sins?
Kids: Everyone sins.

Grown-up: What happens because of our sin?
Kids: We are separated from God forever.

Grown-up: Can we get rid of our sin on our own?
Kids: No!

Grown-up: Who can save us from our sin?
Kids: Jesus!

Grown-up: What should we do to be saved?
Kids: Confess our sin and believe in Jesus as our Savior.

Grown-up: What does it mean to be saved?
Kids: Our sin is forgiven, and we are a part of God's family forever!

PRAY TOGETHER

- **THANK** God that He saves us from our sin.

- **ASK** God to help you understand the good news of the gospel.

Optional: Color all the number 10's on the bonus coloring sheet.
Note: The numbers go through 40. There are 6 spots to color for each number.

PART 3

Memory Verse

If we live by the Spirit,
let us also keep in step
with the Spirit.

GALATIANS 5:25

Walking by the Spirit

MEMORY VERSE

If we live by the Spirit, let us also keep in step with the Spirit.
Galatians 5:25

READ TOGETHER

Galatians 5:16

A few days ago, we learned that when we believe in Jesus and receive His forgiveness, the Holy Spirit comes and lives inside of us. He helps us obey God and gives us the strength not to sin. In Galatians 5, Paul tells us to "walk by the Spirit" and "keep in step with the Spirit."

But how do we know if we're walking by the Spirit? When we obey God's commands in Scripture, we know we're walking by the Spirit. And anytime we put the needs of other people above our own, we know that we are walking by the Spirit. The Spirit will always guide us away from selfishness — thinking only about ourselves — and toward selflessness — thinking about others. That is how Jesus lived, and the Spirit helps us to live like Jesus.

The Spirit helps us to live like Jesus

- Is it hard to think about other people's needs before your own? Why do you think that is?

- Are there any ways we have acted selfishly toward each other this week?

- THANK God for the gift of the Holy Spirit, who helps us to live like Jesus.

- ASK God to help you walk by the Spirit.

Optional: Color all the number 11's on the bonus coloring sheet.
Note: The numbers go through 40. There are 6 spots to color for each number.

Hoping in Jesus

memory verse

If we live by the Spirit, let us also keep in step with the Spirit.
Galatians 5:25

read together

1 Peter 1:3–4

The Bible gives us so many amazing promises! It promises that God will always be with us. It promises that God will take away everything sad about the world. And the Bible also promises that all of God's children will live with Him forever one day. These promises give us hope whenever we feel sad or discouraged because we know that God's promises always come true.

Sometimes when we use the word "hope," we're talking about something we *want* to happen. But when the Bible uses the word "hope," it's talking about something we *know* will happen. When we trust that God will keep His promises, we are putting our hope in Him. Today's verse calls Jesus our "living hope." Because Jesus rose from the dead, we know (or *hope*!) that God's children will be raised with Him and live with Him forever.

God's promises always come true.

- Is there anything that is making you sad this week? How can God's promises help us when we're feeling sad?

- When you think about living with Jesus forever, what are some things that really excite you?

PRAY TOGETHER

- **THANK** Jesus for being our living hope.

- **ASK** God to help you remember His promises when you are discouraged.

Optional: Color all the number 12's on the bonus coloring sheet.
Note: The numbers go through 40. There are 6 spots to color for each number.

Finding Contentment in Christ

MEMORY VERSE

If we live by the Spirit, let us also keep in step with the Spirit.
Galatians 5:25

READ TOGETHER

Philippians 4:10–13

Sometimes we don't get what we want. And it's okay to feel sad or disappointed when that happens! But sometimes, when we don't get what we want, we can become discontent. We can start to think about all that God *hasn't* given us rather than being thankful for what He *has* given us. Yet Paul teaches us in Philippians 4:10–13 that we can be content both when times are great and when times are hard. How? By looking to Jesus!

Jesus gives us the strength to be content in any situation. Being content means that even when we don't get what we want, we know we have everything we need because Jesus forgives our sins, gives us peace with God, and promises to live with us forever in a world with no sadness — only happiness.

Jesus gives us the strength to be content in any situation.

- Can you think of a time when you didn't get what you wanted? How did you respond?

- What are some things God has given our family that we can be thankful for?

PRAY TOGETHER

- **THANK** God for providing all that we need through Jesus.

- **ASK** God to help you be content, even when things don't go your way.

Optional: Color all the number 13's on the bonus coloring sheet.

Note: The numbers go through 40. There are 6 spots to color for each number.

Jesus Understands Us

MEMORY VERSE

If we live by the Spirit, let us also keep in step with the Spirit.
Galatians 5:25

READ TOGETHER

Hebrews 4:14–16

Sometimes when we're sad, it's nice to have someone put their arms around us and give us a hug. It's also nice when someone says, "I know exactly how you feel." And that's exactly what Jesus says to us. He knows what it's like to be us because even though Jesus is God, He came and lived in our world as a human being. Like us, Jesus knows what it's like to be hungry, thirsty, and tired. He knows what it's like to feel lonely and be teased. And He knows what it's like to be tempted to sin. But amazingly, Jesus never sinned!

This means that whenever we're having a hard day, or anytime we want to sin, we can run to Jesus. He gets it! He knows what we're going through, He understands us, and He can help us. So talk to Jesus!

Whenever we're having a hard day, or anytime we want to sin, we can run to Jesus.

ANSWER TOGETHER

- Why can we go to Jesus when we're tempted to sin?

- How does it make you feel to know that Jesus understands what you're going through?

PRAY TOGETHER

- THANK Jesus for becoming human so that He could experience what we experience.

- ASK Jesus to encourage you when you feel sad and give you strength when you're tempted to sin.

Optional: Color all the number 14's on the bonus coloring sheet.

Note: The numbers go through 40. There are 6 spots to color for each number.

Jesus Is Gentle Toward Us

MEMORY VERSE

If we live by the Spirit, let us also keep in step with the Spirit.
Galatians 5:25

READ TOGETHER

Proverbs 15:1

A lot of times, when people get angry, they get louder. Imagine two people who are angry at each other. One gets loud, which makes the other person get louder, which then makes the first person get *even* louder — and so on! When we respond to anger with more anger, things get worse. This is what today's verse means by being "harsh." When we're harsh with others, we use our words to hurt them.

But Jesus is "gentle and humble in heart" (Matthew 11:29, NIV). That means we, too, should be gentle, not harsh. This isn't always easy, but remember: Jesus makes us new! We have new hearts that are able to be gentle and kind. Sometimes it's easy to be harsh and become upset with people. But with the Spirit's help, we can choose to imitate Jesus by being gentle instead.

With the Spirit's help, we can choose to imitate Jesus by being gentle.

ANSWER TOGETHER

- What is an example of being harsh?

- How can our family be gentle like Jesus instead of being harsh?

PRAY TOGETHER

- **THANK** God for the gentleness He shows to us.

- **ASK** for God's strength to help us be gentle with others, not harsh.

Optional: Color all the number 15's on the bonus coloring sheet.
Note: The numbers go through 40. There are 6 spots to color for each number.

Gospel Talk

If we live by the Spirit, let us also keep in step with the Spirit.
Galatians 5:25

Let's practice speaking the gospel to one another. Why? Because the gospel is the best news we could ever hear! And the more we talk about it, the better we will understand just how wonderful it is!

Grown-up: Who sins?
Kids: Everyone sins.

Grown-up: What happens because of our sin?
Kids: We are separated from God forever.

Grown-up: Can we get rid of our sin on our own?
Kids: No!

Grown-up: Who can save us from our sin?
Kids: Jesus!

Grown-up: What should we do to be saved?
Kids: Confess our sin and believe in Jesus as our Savior.

Grown-up: What does it mean to be saved?
Kids: Our sin is forgiven, and we are a part of God's family forever!

PRAY TOGETHER

- **THANK** God that He saves us from our sin.

- **ASK** God to help you understand the good news of the gospel.

Optional: Color all the number 16's on the bonus coloring sheet.
Note: The numbers go through 40. There are 6 spots to color for each number.

PART 4

Memory Verse

So God created man
in his own image;
he created him in the
image of God; he created
them male and female.

GENESIS 1:27

Treating Others as Image-Bearers

MEMORY VERSE

So God created man in his own image; he created him in the image of God; he created them male and female.
Genesis 1:27

READ TOGETHER

Genesis 1:26–27, Luke 6:31

Of all the things God made, the best thing He made was people. That's because God created us in His image. We are image-bearers. This means that God made us to be like Him through the ways we think, behave, and speak. Because all people are made in God's image, every single person you meet is special, valuable, and very important to God!

Knowing this, we should treat everyone with kindness, love, and respect. We should see people the way God sees them and treat them just like God would treat them. This can be hard! But we know that when we are kind to others and show love to them, it makes God really happy. If other people are important to God, they should be important to us as well!

If other people are important to God, they should be important to us as well!

- Why are people so important to God?

- Is it ever hard to be kind to others? How can we treat others as image-bearers this week?

- **THANK** God for creating us in His image.

- **ASK** for God's help to see people the way that He sees them.

Optional: Color all the number 17's on the bonus coloring sheet.

Note: The numbers go through 40. There are 6 spots to color for each number.

Loving Others

MEMORY VERSE

So God created man in his own image; he created him in
the image of God; he created them male and female.
Genesis 1:27

READ TOGETHER

1 John 4:10–11

Yesterday, we talked about how all people are made in God's image and are very important to Him. Because of this, we should love people like God loves them. God showed His love for us by sending Jesus to die for our sins so that we could be forgiven and live forever with Him. God gave us the forgiveness we needed even though we didn't deserve it.

There are lots of ways we can show love to others. We can give them something they need or something we think they'd enjoy. We can spend time with them. Most importantly, we can tell them about how God loved them by sending Jesus. Even when people upset or annoy us, we can still choose to love them, remembering that God loved us when we didn't deserve His love!

God showed His love for us by sending Jesus to die for our sins.

- Why is it important to love others?

- Who are some people we can show love to as a family this week?

- **THANK** God for loving you, even when you didn't deserve it!

- **ASK** God to help you love other people the way He has loved you.

Optional: Color all the number 18's on the bonus coloring sheet.

Note: The numbers go through 40. There are 6 spots to color for each number.

Keeping from Complaining

MEMORY VERSE

So God created man in his own image; he created him in
the image of God; he created them male and female.
Genesis 1:27

READ TOGETHER

Philippians 2:14–15

Sometimes, when we don't get what we want, we complain. God's people, the Israelites, complained a lot in the Bible! In the book of Exodus, God rescued the Israelites from Egypt, where they had been slaves, and promised to bring them to a beautiful new home. But first, they had to travel through a desert to get there! Instead of trusting God to give them food and water, they complained. They felt like God wouldn't take care of them, even though He had just rescued them from Egypt!

We, too, can forget that God knows what's best for us and that God's plans for us are always good. Since He has rescued us from our sin through Jesus, we know that we can trust Him to take care of us, and this keeps us from complaining. Instead of complaining, let's trust that God loves us and will take care of us!

- What are some things that you complain about?

- How can we remind each other that God cares for us?

- **THANK** God for taking care of us and giving us what we need.

- **ASK** for God's forgiveness for when we complain.

Optional: Color all the number 19's on the bonus coloring sheet.

Note: The numbers go through 40. There are 6 spots to color for each number.

Being a Cheerful Giver

MEMORY VERSE

So God created man in his own image; he created him in
the image of God; he created them male and female.

Genesis 1:27

READ TOGETHER

2 Corinthians 9:7

God loves when we share. But sharing can be hard! Sometimes, we would rather keep something for ourselves and not share it. But when we act selfishly, we are forgetting something important: everything we have is a gift from God! And God gives us these gifts not just for ourselves but also to share with others.

Jesus once told a rich young ruler to sell everything he owned, give to the poor, and then follow Jesus (Luke 18:18–23). But the ruler went away sad because he didn't want to give away his stuff! Like this man, we can also struggle to give things away. But the gospel reminds us that Jesus gave everything for us. He died on the cross so that we can be saved. Jesus is the best giver, and when we remember Him, we are encouraged to give. So let's be cheerful givers and live with open hands!

The gospel reminds us that Jesus gave everything for us.

- Why is it important to share what we have with others?

- What are some things that we could give away to help others?

- THANK Jesus for cheerfully dying on the cross for our sins.

- ASK God to help you to cheerfully share what you have with others.

Optional: Color all the number 20's on the bonus coloring sheet.

Note: The numbers go through 40. There are 6 spots to color for each number.

Listening to Authority

So God created man in his own image; he created him in
the image of God; he created them male and female.

Genesis 1:27

Ephesians 6:1–3

Do you know what authority means? It means being in charge! There are lots of authority figures in our lives: parents, teachers, and police officers. People in authority give us rules to obey and make decisions to help us. But even they should listen to God and do what He says. God tells authority figures to care for us, and He wants us to obey them. Putting authority figures in our lives is one way that God cares for us.

So, when we disobey our parents or our teachers, it's like we are also disobeying God since He put them in charge of us to help us. But God is very happy when we listen to them, obey them, and show them patience when they make mistakes! God uses these people to care for us, and by honoring them, we also honor God.

Putting authority figures in our lives is one way that God cares for us.

ANSWER TOGETHER

- Who are some authority figures in our lives?

- Why is it important to listen to these people?

PRAY TOGETHER

- **THANK** God for the authorities in your life who care for you.

- **ASK** for God's help to listen to authorities and obey them.

Optional: Color all the number 21's on the bonus coloring sheet.

Note: The numbers go through 40. There are 6 spots to color for each number.

Gospel Talk

memory verse

So God created man in his own image; he created him in
the image of God; he created them male and female

Genesis 1:27

Let's practice speaking the gospel to one another. Why? Because the
gospel is the best news we could ever hear! And the more we talk about
it, the better we will understand just how wonderful it is!

Grown-up: Who sins?
Kids: Everyone sins.

Grown-up: What happens because of our sin?
Kids: We are separated from God forever.

Grown-up: Can we get rid of our sin on our own?
Kids: No!

Grown-up: Who can save us from our sin?
Kids: Jesus!

Grown-up: What should we do to be saved?
Kids: Confess our sin and believe in Jesus as our Savior.

Grown-up: What does it mean to be saved?
Kids: Our sin is forgiven, and we are a part of God's family forever!

PRAY TOGETHER

- **THANK** God that He saves us from our sin.

- **ASK** God to help you understand the good news of the gospel.

Optional: Color all the number 22's on the bonus coloring sheet.
Note: The numbers go through 40. There are 6 spots to color for each number.

PART 5

Memory Verse

If possible, as far as it
depends on you, live at
peace with everyone.

ROMANS 12:18

Being Peaceful

If possible, as far as it depends on you, live at peace with everyone.
Romans 12:18

Romans 12:18

The Bible says that when our sins are forgiven through Jesus, we have peace with God. What does it mean to have peace with God? This peace is a feeling of calm and security that comes because our relationship with God has been made right. Even though we had disobeyed Him and made Him sad because of our sin, God still came to us, in Christ, because He wanted to give us peace with Himself. And because God loves peace, He wants us to share peace with others, too!

How can we be peaceful people? We can do this by trying to make our relationships with others right! We can avoid fighting or arguing with others. We can choose to be patient and kind when someone makes us upset. And when we do something wrong to someone else, we can go to them and tell them how sorry we are. All of this can be very hard to do! But when we make peace with others, we are imitating God, who made peace with us.

When we make peace with others, we are acting like God, who made peace with us.

- When is it hard to be peaceful people?

- Is there anyone we need to make peace with this week?

- **THANK** God for offering peace to us, even when we didn't deserve it!

- **ASK** for God's help to offer peace to others and to not be unkind.

Optional: Color all the number 23's on the bonus coloring sheet.

Note: The numbers go through 40. There are 6 spots to color for each number.

Living Honestly

MEMORY VERSE
If possible, as far as it depends on you, live at peace with everyone.
Romans 12:18

READ TOGETHER
Ephesians 4:25, Colossians 3:9–10a

The Bible tells us that God never lies (Numbers 23:19). And because He doesn't lie, He doesn't want us to lie either. Lying keeps us from being honest, and being honest is important because the truth is important. Speaking the truth to each other helps us learn and grow. But lying keeps us from being who God created us to be. Lying only hurts us and those around us.

Sometimes, we lie because we feel like we have to hide something. But if we believe in Jesus, we don't have to hide anything from God. God knows everything about us and still loves us. Since God accepts us, we don't have to pretend to be someone we're not! And if we're honest with God, we can be honest with others. So when we feel like we want to lie, let's remember the forgiveness Jesus gives us and be honest instead.

God knows everything about us and still loves us.

ANSWER TOGETHER

- Why is it sometimes hard to tell the truth?

- How can we encourage each other to be more honest?

PRAY TOGETHER

- **THANK** God that because of His grace and forgiveness, we don't have to hide anything from Him.

- **ASK** God to help you be honest and avoid lying.

Optional: Color all the number 24's on the bonus coloring sheet.

Note: The numbers go through 40. There are 6 spots to color for each number.

Having Patience

MEMORY VERSE

If possible, as far as it depends on you, live at peace with everyone.
Romans 12:18

READ TOGETHER

Ephesians 4:1–2

Most people don't like waiting. It makes us impatient! Impatience means that instead of waiting in a calm way, we start to feel frustrated and upset. Whatever we're waiting for, we'd rather have it *now*!

Impatience leads to problems. It can lead us to avoid being kind to others. If we feel someone is taking too long to do something, we might be mean to them by telling them to hurry up. We might yell when someone does something the wrong way. Impatience can also show us that we're only thinking of ourselves. Usually, we get impatient because we want things to happen the way we want them to happen.

But God calls us to be patient and think of others. Jesus is patient with us, and He helps us to have patience with others, even in difficult moments. So we can ask for Jesus's help when we start to feel impatient.

Jesus is patient with us, and He helps us to have patience with others, even in difficult moments.

- Can you think of a time recently when you were impatient? How did you react?

- Why is it important to remember that God is patient with us?

- **THANK** God for the patience He shows us.

- **ASK** for help to be patient with others the way God is patient with us.

Optional: Color all the number 25's on the bonus coloring sheet.

Note: The numbers go through 40. There are 6 spots to color for each number.

Dealing with Anger

If possible, as far as it depends on you, live at peace with everyone.
Romans 12:18

READ TOGETHER

James 1:19–20

Some things usually go together, like peanut butter and jelly or macaroni and cheese. Anger and sin often go together, too. Bad things often happen when we're angry. We say mean things. We hurt people. We can think mean thoughts about them. Sometimes we think it's okay to be angry if someone does something that bothers us. But even then, we should avoid anger because, as today's verse says, anger doesn't bring about God's righteousness.

We bring about God's righteousness by obeying God. We obey God by doing things that please Him and that bring help to others. But in our anger, we're usually not thinking of how to help others! We need God's help because it is so easy to become angry. Thankfully, God gives us His Holy Spirit to help us avoid anger and live in ways that please Him and help others.

We bring about God's righteousness by obeying God.

- When was the last time you were angry? Did you disobey God while you were angry?

- How can we respond to our anger in ways that please God?

- **THANK** God for forgiving us even though we have given Him lots of reasons to be angry with us.

- **ASK** for His help to control our anger and seek the good of others.

Optional: Color all the number 26's on the bonus coloring sheet.

Note: The numbers go through 40. There are 6 spots to color for each number.

Not Judging Others

If possible, as far as it depends on you, live at peace with everyone.
Romans 12:18

John 7:24

During Jesus's life, there was a group of people called the Pharisees who didn't like Him. The Pharisees had come up with new rules for how to obey God's commands, and they thought they were better than people who didn't follow their rules. For example, they thought that one way to obey God was to avoid people who seemed to be really bad sinners. Since Jesus chose to be around sinners, the Pharisees thought that He must not love God! They were judging Jesus.

When we judge others like this, we assume that we are better than them. And this is usually for silly reasons! Maybe we judge people because of what they wear, what they look like, or who their friends are. But Jesus tells us not to judge others. Instead, we should get to know them, treat them with kindness, and remember that they are very important to God.

Jesus tells us not to judge others.

- What does it mean to judge others? Why is it wrong?

- Are there ways that we tend to judge other people?

- **THANK** God for the grace He shows us through Jesus.

- **ASK** God to help you see people as He sees them and love people as He loves them.

Optional: Color all the number 27's on the bonus coloring sheet.
Note: The numbers go through 40. There are 6 spots to color for each number.

Gospel Talk

If possible, as far as it depends on you, live at peace with everyone.
Romans 12:18

Let's practice speaking the gospel to one another. Why? Because the gospel is the best news we could ever hear! And the more we talk about it, the better we will understand just how wonderful it is!

Grown-up: Who sins?
Kids: Everyone sins.

Grown-up: What happens because of our sin?
Kids: We are separated from God forever.

Grown-up: Can we get rid of our sin on our own?
Kids: No!

Grown-up: Who can save us from our sin?
Kids: Jesus!

Grown-up: What should we do to be saved?
Kids: Confess our sin and believe in Jesus as our Savior.

Grown-up: What does it mean to be saved?
Kids: Our sin is forgiven, and we are a part of God's family forever!

PRAY TOGETHER

- **THANK** God that He saves us from our sin.

- **ASK** God to help you understand the good news of the gospel.

Optional: Color all the number 28's on the bonus coloring sheet.
Note: The numbers go through 40. There are 6 spots to color for each number.

PART 6

Memory Verse

Imitate me, as I also
imitate Christ.

1 CORINTHIANS 11:1

Not Being Jealous

Imitate me, as I also imitate Christ.

1 Corinthians 11:1

James 3:14–16

On Day 13, we talked about being content, which means being happy with what God has given us. But when we are discontent, we complain about what God *hasn't* given us instead of being thankful for what He has given us. Being jealous is like being discontent. When we're jealous, we aren't content with what we have, and we want what someone else has. Maybe someone else has a toy you wish you had. Maybe other people think they're funnier than you. These things can make us jealous.

Sometimes, we want what someone else has so that we can feel better about ourselves. But Jesus tells us that we are loved and forgiven no matter what we have or don't have. So we don't need anything else to make us feel happy or better about ourselves. Jesus gives us what we really need: peace with God. We are very important to God, and knowing this is better than anything else we can have!

Jesus tells us that we are loved and forgiven no matter what we have or don't have.

- What makes you jealous?

- What are some good things that Jesus gives us?

- THANK God for giving us all we really need.

- ASK God to help us not grow jealous over what we don't have but to focus on what we do have.

Optional: Color all the number 29's on the bonus coloring sheet.

Note: The numbers go through 40. There are 6 spots to color for each number.

Fighting Laziness

Imitate me, as I also imitate Christ.
1 Corinthians 11:1

Colossians 3:23–24

The Bible tells us that we should be like ants (Proverbs 6:6–8). Why? Because they aren't lazy! Laziness is different from rest. When we rest, we're taking a break after working hard and fulfilling our responsibilities. But when we're lazy, we don't want to work hard, and we avoid our responsibilities.

Laziness keeps us from using our time well. When we're lazy, we're focused on what is easiest or most comfortable for *us* and not on what is helpful for others. But God calls us to serve Him and care for people. When we do this, we act like Jesus, who did the hard work of loving others, obeying God, and dying on the cross for our sins. Jesus makes us new and gives us strength to fight laziness and work hard for God and others.

Jesus makes us new and gives us strength to fight laziness and work hard for God and others.

- Why is laziness bad? How is it different from rest?

- What are some ways that we are sometimes lazy as a family? How can we work hard instead?

PRAY TOGETHER

- **THANK** God for forgiving us when we're lazy.

- **ASK** for God's help to not be lazy but to work hard to serve Him and others!

Optional: Color all the number 30's on the bonus coloring sheet.

Note: The numbers go through 40. There are 6 spots to color for each number.

Speaking Gracious Words

MEMORY VERSE

Imitate me, as I also imitate Christ.
1 Corinthians 11:1

READ TOGETHER

Ephesians 4:29, Colossians 4:6

God cares a lot about how we talk to other people. Why? Because our words have a big effect on them! Kind words can make someone happy, while mean words can hurt their feelings. But God wants us to use our words to help people. When we use our words to help others, we are speaking graciously to them. To speak graciously means to speak with kindness and compassion and to help people feel loved. When we do this, we're imitating Jesus!

But speaking graciously also sometimes means telling people things they don't want to hear. When someone is doing something wrong or dangerous, the loving thing is to warn them to stop. But even then, we can be kind and gracious in how we talk to them. It's not always easy to speak graciously, but fortunately, we have the Holy Spirit, who helps us use our words to help others!

We have the Holy Spirit, who helps us use our words to help others!

▪ Why does God care about how we use our words?

▪ What are some ways we can speak gracious words to others?

▪ **THANK** God for giving us the Spirit, who helps us speak the way Jesus speaks.

▪ **ASK** God to help you speak gracious words to others.

Optional: Color all the number 31's on the bonus coloring sheet.
Note: The numbers go through 40. There are 6 spots to color for each number.

Putting On Jesus's Character

MEMORY VERSE

Imitate me, as I also imitate Christ.
1 Corinthians 11:1

READ TOGETHER

Colossians 3:12–15

The Bible says that if we follow Jesus, we should start to look like Jesus! Our words should sound like the words He would say. Our behavior should look like ways He would behave. Today's passage tells us to "put on" Jesus's characteristics like we would put on clothes! We should also take off any behaviors that aren't like Jesus, just like we would take off dirty clothes.

Putting on Jesus's character means choosing to obey God with the Holy Spirit's help instead of doing what is sinful. And it's something that we should do each day. When we choose to be kind to someone instead of becoming angry or when we choose to be patient instead of becoming impatient, we're putting on these characteristics of Jesus. Sometimes, this is really hard to do! But when we do so, we will look more like Him, which is what the Christian life is all about!

Putting on Jesus's character means choosing to obey God with the Holy Spirit's help instead of doing what is sinful.

- Why is it important to behave like Jesus?

- What are some ways we can "put on" Jesus this week?

- **THANK** God for Jesus, who never sinned and who gives us the strength to live like Him.

- **ASK** for God's help to put on Jesus and put off sin.

Optional: Color all the number 32's on the bonus coloring sheet.

Note: The numbers go through 40. There are 6 spots to color for each number.

Forgiving Like Jesus

MEMORY VERSE

Imitate me, as I also imitate Christ.
1 Corinthians 11:1

READ TOGETHER

Matthew 18:21–22

When someone hurts us or upsets us, we might feel angry or sad. And it can be hard to forgive them. We might even think they don't deserve our forgiveness. But God calls us to forgive others, even if they keep messing up.

In Matthew 18, Jesus tells the story of a servant who owed his master some money but couldn't pay it back (Matthew 18:23–35). Thankfully, the master forgave the servant and told him he didn't have to pay him back. The servant was so happy! But then, the servant met someone who owed *him* a very small amount of money and couldn't pay it. Instead of doing what his master had just done for him, the servant threw that man in jail!

Jesus's point is that we should remember how much God has forgiven us — even when we didn't deserve it! — and show that same forgiveness to others.

God calls us to forgive others, even if they keep messing up.

- Why is it hard to forgive? Why should we forgive others?

- Is there someone you need to forgive?

PRAY TOGETHER

- **THANK** God for forgiving us through Jesus, even though we didn't deserve it!

- **ASK** God to help us forgive others the way we have been forgiven.

Optional: Color all the number 33's on the bonus coloring sheet.
Note: The numbers go through 40. There are 6 spots to color for each number.

Gospel Talk

memory verse

Imitate me, as I also imitate Christ.

1 Corinthians 11:1

Let's practice speaking the gospel to one another. Why? Because the gospel is the best news we could ever hear! And the more we talk about it, the better we will understand just how wonderful it is!

Grown-up: Who sins?
Kids: Everyone sins.

Grown-up: What happens because of our sin?
Kids: We are separated from God forever.

Grown-up: Can we get rid of our sin on our own?
Kids: No!

Grown-up: Who can save us from our sin?
Kids: Jesus!

Grown-up: What should we do to be saved?
Kids: Confess our sin and believe in Jesus as our Savior.

Grown-up: What does it mean to be saved?
Kids: Our sin is forgiven, and we are a part of God's family forever!

PRAY TOGETHER

- **THANK** God that He saves us from our sin.

- **ASK** God to help you understand the good news of the gospel.

Optional: Color all the number 34's on the bonus coloring sheet.
Note: The numbers go through 40. There are 6 spots to color for each number.

PART 7

Memory Verse

But God proves his own
love for us in that while
we were still sinners,
Christ died for us.

ROMANS 5:8

Caring Like Jesus

But God proves his own love for us in that while
we were still sinners, Christ died for us.
Romans 5:8

Luke 10:29–37

Of all the commands God gives us in the Bible, Jesus said that the most important ones were to love God with our whole heart and to love our neighbor (Luke 10:25–28). But who is our "neighbor"? When Jesus was asked this question, He told the story of the Good Samaritan. In this story, a man is robbed and hurt, and afterward, two people walk past him without stopping to help him. But a third man walks by and stops, takes care of the man, and finds a place for him to rest.

Who is our neighbor? Jesus's answer is: *everyone*! And since everyone is our neighbor, we're to love all people. We should imitate Jesus, who cared for the people He met and who even died on the cross so that people could receive God's forgiveness. As we think about how Jesus loved us, let's show that love to others.

As we think about how Jesus loved us, let's show that love to others.

- Why is it important to care for others?

- Who is someone you can care for this week?

- **THANK** God for showing compassion to us when we were in need.

- **ASK** God to forgive us for the times we don't show compassion to others, and ask Him for strength to show compassion to those around us.

Optional: Color all the number 35's on the bonus coloring sheet.
Note: The numbers go through 40. There are 6 spots to color for each number.

Jesus Frees Us

But God proves his own love for us in that while
we were still sinners, Christ died for us
Romans 5:8

Romans 6:22–23

The Bible says that everyone has sinned. In fact, it says that we are like prisoners of sin! But Jesus came to set us free from being sin's prisoners and to help us fight against sin. When someone frees us, we should thank them, and one way we thank Jesus for rescuing us from being prisoners of sin is by living for Him. Living for Jesus means loving Him, obeying His commands, and acting like Him.

Being set free from sin doesn't mean we will never sin again. It means that we have the freedom *not* to sin and also that Jesus took the punishment for our sin. Through the Holy Spirit, Jesus gives us the strength to obey Him. And we obey Him with love, joy, and thankfulness because of what He has done to rescue us.

Living for Jesus means loving Him, obeying His commands, and acting like Him.

- Who sets us free from sin?

- How can we live for Jesus as a family?

PRAY TOGETHER

- **THANK** Jesus for dying on the cross to set us free from sin.

- **ASK** God to help us as we continue to fight against sin.

Optional: Color all the number 36's on the bonus coloring sheet.

Note: The numbers go through 40. There are 6 spots to color for each number.

Jesus Strengthens Us

MEMORY VERSE

But God proves his own love for us in that while
we were still sinners, Christ died for us.
Romans 5:8

READ TOGETHER
2 Peter 1:3

Have you ever tried to carry something that was too heavy for you?
Sometimes, we're not strong enough to carry things on our own, so
we ask someone to help us. This is important to remember when we
fight against sin, because trying to fight sin by ourselves is like trying
to lift something that is too heavy. We need help! By ourselves, we're
not strong enough to stop sinning and obey Jesus.

But God gives us help to fight sin by sending us the Holy Spirit. God
gives us the help we need to obey Him. So we can ask God to help us
love Him and run from sin, knowing that He will give us everything
we need to do that! Through Jesus, we receive the strength we need
to live in ways that please God.

Through Jesus, we receive the strength we need to live in ways that please God.

- Why can't we fight sin on our own?

- Who gives us the power to fight sin?

PRAY TOGETHER

- **THANK** God for giving us the strength we need to fight against sin.

- **ASK** God to give you the strength to live in ways that please Him every day!

Optional: Color all the number 37's on the bonus coloring sheet.

Note: The numbers go through 40. There are 6 spots to color for each number.

Jesus Forgives Us

MEMORY VERSE

But God proves his own love for us in that while
we were still sinners, Christ died for us.
Romans 5:8

READ TOGETHER

Ephesians 1:7

The Bible says that God removes our sins as far as the east is from the west (Psalm 103:12). That's really far! Just as the east is miles and miles away from the west, God's forgiveness keeps on going and going.

Sometimes when we sin, we might wonder, *Does God still forgive me?* The good news is that if we believe in Jesus, He will always forgive us. When Jesus died on the cross, He was punished for all the bad things we've ever done. This should encourage us when we sin. Whenever we mess up, we don't have to worry about God not forgiving us. So even on our worst days, we can know that we're forgiven. Thanks to Jesus, God's forgiveness keeps on going and going forever!

Grown-up: Who sins?
Kids: Everyone sins.

Grown-up: What happens because of our sin?
Kids: We are separated from God forever.

Grown-up: Can we get rid of our sin on our own?
Kids: No!

Grown-up: Who can save us from our sin?
Kids: Jesus!

Grown-up: What should we do to be saved?
Kids: Confess our sin and believe in Jesus as our Savior.

Grown-up: What does it mean to be saved?
Kids: Our sin is forgiven, and we are a part of God's family forever!

PRAY TOGETHER

- **THANK** God that He saves us from our sin.

- **ASK** God to help you understand the good news of the gospel.

Optional: Color all the number 40's on the bonus coloring sheet.
Note: The numbers go through 40. There are 6 spots to color for each number.

GLOSSARY

CONFESS:
Being honest with God about your thoughts, feelings, or actions — whether they are good or bad

ETERNAL LIFE:
Living forever in God's presence

FAITH:
Trusting that Jesus can save you from your sin

FORGIVENESS:
Releasing someone from the wrong they've done

GOSPEL:
The good news that salvation comes by grace and through faith in Jesus

GRACE:
God giving us what we don't deserve through Christ

HOLY:
Being set apart and pure

MERCY:
God's great kindness and forgiveness

OLD TESTAMENT:
The first part of the Bible that records God's rules, the history of Israel, and God's promises of Jesus

PEACE:
A feeling of calm and security that comes from having our relationship with God and others made right

SACRIFICE:
An animal or object given to God to pay the price for sin

SALVATION:
God rescuing sinners from sin

SATAN:
God's enemy, whose mission is to separate people from God for eternity

SCRIPTURE/GOD'S WORD:
The Bible; God's truth written down for us to obey

SIN:
Thoughts, actions, and beliefs that go against God's rules and ways

HOW TO MAKE TIME FOR FAMILY DEVOTIONS

Family life is always busy! We are often juggling school, work, extra-curricular activities, appointments, and so much more. How can we make time for family devotions in the midst of all that we have on our calendars? The answer may be more simple than you think. Below are three steps that will help you make the time!

STEP 1: PICK A TIME

On average, a devotion in *Jesus Makes Me New* takes around ten to fifteen minutes to complete. When does your family have ten to fifteen minutes to spare? Is it in the mornings before everyone takes off for work and school? During mealtime? Or before bed? Pick a time that will work best. It may not work perfectly every day, and that's okay. You may pick a time and then end up changing it when seasons and commitments change, and that's also okay. There is no such thing as the perfect time! Just start with what will work best for now, and remain flexible yet committed to your family devotion time.

STEP 2: COMMUNICATE

Let everyone in the family know you will be spending ten to fifteen minutes a day doing a family devotion together at the time you have chosen. This may mean family members need to slightly alter their

OVERCOMING CHALLENGES

Below are some common challenges parents and caregivers face when teaching their children about God and the Bible. If and when you experience any of these, feel free to refer back to these pages for encouragement!

MY KIDS AREN'T PAYING ATTENTION. ARE THEY EVEN LEARNING ANYTHING?

Kids have very short attention spans and are easily distracted. We understand how that can make you wonder if it's even worth it to put effort into a family devotion time. It is not likely your kids will remember every little thing they are taught. But it is likely that they will remember something, and often they will recall more than you think! Teaching children about God is a marathon, not a sprint. It's a race you will likely run alongside your children for decades. The goal isn't for your children to have perfect retention today but to faithfully and consistently teach them for a lifetime. Don't be discouraged by their wandering minds. Instead, be patient with them, trusting that even when they are distracted, it does not stop the Holy Spirit from working in their hearts and minds.

Scripture: Isaiah 55:10–11

I DON'T FEEL EQUIPPED TO TEACH THE BIBLE TO MY KIDS.

The Bible is a big, long, and sometimes confusing book. It's completely normal to feel intimidated by the task of teaching your children the truth it holds. Be encouraged that you do not need to be an expert to lead your family in the pursuit of God. It is okay if you feel confused about passages of Scripture or theological concepts. You can be honest with your children and say, "I'm not sure what that means, but we can figure it out together." A good study Bible such as the *ESV Study Bible* or the *NIV Biblical Theology Study Bible* would be a great place to start if you want to dive deeper into certain verses or concepts.

Scripture: 2 Peter 1:3

my spouse and I aren't on the same page.

A common challenge to teaching children about God is when your spouse is not on the same page as you. They may be apathetic about faith conversations, or they may be completely opposed to them. While every family is different, and we cannot tell you how to handle this situation amid your unique family dynamics, there are a few things you may want to consider trying. First, pray for unity between you and your spouse. Pray for the Holy Spirit to do a deep inner work in your spouse's heart and grow an affection for God and His Word in him or her. Second, let your spouse know about your plan for a family devotion time; invite them to take part in it, but do not pressure them to join. Third, be flexible. Your spouse may feel like your family devotion time is causing division in the family. Consider shortening your family devotion time or incorporating something like a craft or game in which they can participate.

Scripture: 1 Corinthians 7:12–16

TIPS FOR HELPING CHILDREN MEMORIZE SCRIPTURE

- Create actions to go along with each word or phrase.

- Practice a few times a day. Some great times to practice are during meals, in the car, and before bed.

- Write the first letter of each word in the verse on a sticky note, and use it as a cheat sheet until the verse is memorized.

- Post the verse in a visible place, like on the bathroom mirror or refrigerator.

- Sing the verse to the tune of a familiar song.

- Have children look up the verse in the Bible and read it independently.

- Keep track of verses memorized, and practice them once a week to promote long-term memory.

- Use resources from The Daily Grace Co.®, such as the *Scripture Memory Journal* for kids or the *Daily He Leads Me* notepad for kids. You can find these resources at www.thedailygraceco.com.

SHARING THE GOOD NEWS OF THE GOSPEL WITH CHILDREN

Many people begin their relationship with Jesus at a young age. Throughout this devotional, the good news of the gospel is presented. Children may understand their sin and need for a Savior for the first time during this devotional. Grown-ups, you may want to ask your children if they want to decide to believe in Jesus and receive forgiveness for their sins. It is important not to pressure children to make this decision, but it is also important to lead them to Christ if they are ready.

We suggest asking your children the following questions to start a conversation about the gospel.

What do you think about today's devotion?

Do you think Jesus died to forgive your sins?

*Are you ready to ask forgiveness for your sins
and tell Jesus you believe in Him?*

Listen to your child's answers, and encourage them if they say they want to repent and believe. If your child expresses their belief in Jesus and a desire to trust Him as their Savior, you may want to help them communicate their repentance and belief to God.

When your child is ready to respond to the gospel message, there is no specific prayer to pray or formula to follow. The Bible never actually presents us with a prayer that leads to salvation. Instead, Jesus often calls people to believe (John 6:35) and follow Him (Matthew 19:21). And the apostles teach us to "confess with your mouth, 'Jesus is Lord,' and believe in your heart that God raised him from the dead" to be saved (Romans 10:9).

Scripture demonstrates that salvation is an issue of the heart. It is not the words you say but the belief in your heart that leads to salvation. Salvation is the work of God in response to one's faith in Christ.

However, a natural overflow of believing in God is praying to Him. And what better moment to pray to Him than in the moment you realize the depth of your sin and your need for a Savior? Praying with your child in response to the gospel is a sincere conversation between a repentant sinner and a gracious God, not a spoken script to receive salvation. However, you could lead them in a prayer that goes something like this:

God, I've sinned against You, and I know that I can never make this right on my own. I trust that Jesus's sacrifice was enough to bring me into a real, life-changing relationship with You. Redeem my life, Lord. I can't do it apart from You. I am making the choice to walk with You in my mind, heart, and actions every day, and I want to start today. Amen.

There is nothing magical about these words. They simply communicate the admission of sin and belief in God's saving power. Salvation is an issue of the heart. If your child chooses to repent of their sin and believe in Jesus, celebrate this wonderful moment with them! Tell them they have made an amazing decision, and they are now part of God's family!

BIBLIOGRAPHY

Turner, Shelby. *All About Jesus: A Family Devotional*. Hanover, MD: The Daily Grace Co., 2022.

Thank you for studying God's Word with us!

CONNECT WITH US
@thedailygraceco
@dailygracepodcast

CONTACT US
info@thedailygraceco.com

SHARE
#thedailygraceco

VISIT US ONLINE
www.thedailygraceco.com

MORE DAILY GRACE
Daily Grace® Podcast